50 THINGS YOU SHOULD KNOW ABOUT SPACE

by Professor Raman Prinja

QED

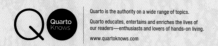

Quarto is the authority on a wide range of topics.
Quarto educates, entertains and enriches the lives of
our readers—enthusiasts and lovers of hands-on living.
www.quartoknows.com

Publisher: Maxime Boucknooghe
Editorial Director: Victoria Garrard
Art Director: Miranda Snow
Project Editor: Joanna McInerney
Design and Editorial: Tall Tree Ltd

Copyright © QED Publishing 2016

First published in the UK in 2016
by QED Publishing
Part of The Quarto Group
The Old Brewery, 6 Blundell Street
London, N7 9BH

A catalogue record for this book is
available from the British Library.

ISBN 978 1 78493 472 9

Printed in China

Words in **bold** are explained
in the glossary on page 78.

To Kamini, Vikas and Sachin – RKP

CONTENTS

INTRODUCTION

Since the invention of the **telescope** just over 400 years ago, our knowledge of the Universe has grown enormously. Today, **astronomers** can see farther than ever before, studying objects far out in the Universe. Spacecraft have journeyed to distant worlds, and humankind has travelled into space and even set foot on the Moon.

▲ Images such as this one, of two galaxies measuring 180,000 light years across, have helped astronomers to understand the size of space.

VAST DISTANCES

Space is very big. To get an idea of just how big, imagine a scale model where the Sun is the size of a basketball. The Earth would be a pea 32 metres away, while the next star would be another basketball 9,000 kilometres away. It would take 200 billion basketballs just to make a model of our own **Milky Way** galaxy. And there are at least 100 billion galaxies in the Universe.

STUDYING SPACE

Our understanding of the Universe depends on our studying the faint light reaching us from distant parts of our **galaxy** and beyond. To do this, astronomers use powerful telescopes, on the ground and in space, as well as the latest computer and engineering technology.

◄ In the 17th century, Italian scientist Galileo (centre, standing) became one of the first people to study space using a telescope.

▶ The modern successor to Galileo's telescope, the Hubble Space Telescope, orbits the Earth taking images of deep space.

EXPLORING SPACE

To study other worlds in greater detail, scientists have launched numerous spacecraft on amazing voyages across the **Solar System** to explore planets, moons, **comets** and **asteroids**. People have also been sent into space, **orbiting** the Earth, living in space stations for months on end, and even setting foot on the Moon during the **NASA**-run *Apollo* missions. Between 1969 and 1972, 12 **astronauts** visited the Moon, marking humankind's first (and so far only) visits to a world other than the Earth. However, scientists believe it may be possible for astronauts to travel to Mars and back in the future.

▼ *The US astronaut Buzz Aldrin steps down onto the Moon in 1969.*

NEW DISCOVERIES

Astronomers watch the Universe's most powerful events, from **black holes** tearing apart stars to galaxy collisions. Discoveries are being made all the time, such as the thousands of planets orbiting distant stars and the mysterious force of **dark energy** that is believed to be pushing the Universe apart.

▲ *Some of the spectacular images captured by the Hubble Space Telescope in the past few decades.*

The Universe is expanding

The Universe is all of space and everything in it, including galaxies, stars, planets, moons and living things. It is everything we can see and measure, making it almost unimaginably vast – and it's getting bigger all the time. Scientists believe the Universe is still expanding at an ever increasing rate.

Powerful telescopes have allowed us to take images such as this one, showing some of the farthest galaxies, which formed shortly after the Universe began.

BILLIONS OF GALAXIES

It is estimated that there are more than 100 billion galaxies in the Universe. That's the number 1 followed by 11 zeros. And there are on average about 100 billion stars in each galaxy. That means that the number of stars in the Universe is so huge it has to be written down as a 1 followed by 22 zeros. Perhaps even more incredibly, the Universe is so large that even with these vast numbers of galaxies and stars, most of space is empty.

Vast distances
Special units called light years are used to measure the size of space (see page 8).

Big Bang
Scientists believe the Universe expanded from a single point (see page 9).

The Greek astronomer Ptolemy (90–170 CE) came up with a model of the Universe with the Earth at its centre and all the planets and Sun orbiting it. Known as the 'geocentric Universe', this idea lasted for centuries. But in the early 16th century, the Polish astronomer Nicholas Copernicus (1473–1543) devised a new model. After studying the night sky, he placed the Sun at the centre of the Universe, and had the planets orbiting it. This is a 'heliocentric Universe'.

Geocentric Universe

Heliocentric Universe

▲ *Much of our understanding of the Universe is based on the studies of gravity by the English scientist Sir Isaac Newton (1643–1727).*

MOVING APART

The Universe has grown larger and larger since it began around 13.8 billion years ago. Incredibly, the space we see today is almost a billion times bigger than it was when the Universe was very young. As the Universe continues to expand, so the space between galaxies is also being stretched and the galaxies are moving farther away from each other. This is known as an 'expanding Universe'. Neither the Earth nor the Sun lie at its centre, because the Universe does not have a centre.

UNDERSTANDING THE COSMOS

Our understanding of what the Universe is and how it works has improved vastly through the centuries. Over time, astronomers have made better measurements of objects in the sky, built more powerful telescopes and even put some of them in orbit around the Earth. Our knowledge of related subjects, such as physics and mathematics, has also increased.

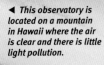

◀ *This observatory is located on a mountain in Hawaii where the air is clear and there is little light pollution.*

Fraction of time
Humans have been around for just a tiny part of the Universe's 13.8-billion-year history (see pages 10–11).

Dark matter
Most of the Universe is made up of the strange, little-understood substance, dark matter (see page 12).

Dark energy
The mysterious force of dark energy is causing the Universe to expand ever more quickly (see page 13).

Bang or whimper?
Scientists have developed several theories about how the Universe might end (see pages 14–15).

Measuring space

Space is huge and the distances between objects in the Universe can be enormous. The Moon is 384,400 kilometres away from us, the Sun is 150 million kilometres from the Earth, and Neptune is 4.5 billion kilometres from the Sun.

The Universe we can see with telescopes has a diameter of 92 billion light years.

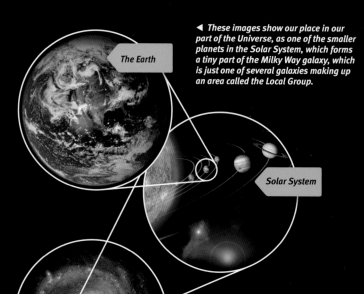

◄ These images show our place in our part of the Universe, as one of the smaller planets in the Solar System, which forms a tiny part of the Milky Way galaxy, which is just one of several galaxies making up an area called the Local Group.

The Earth

Solar System

Milky Way

Local Group

OUR NEAREST NEIGHBOUR

The numbers start to get even more mind-boggling when we go beyond the Solar System. The nearest star to the Sun, Proxima Centauri, is an incredible 41 trillion kilometres away. That's the number 41 followed by 12 zeros. And other stars are much farther away than that.

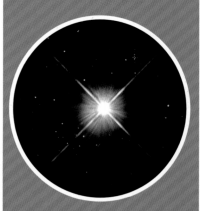

▲ Proxima Centauri, the closest star to our Solar System, is 4.3 light years from the Earth.

LIGHT YEARS

Standard distance units, such as kilometres, are not very useful for measuring space. So astronomers use a special unit called a **light year**. One light year is the distance light travels in one year. Since light has a speed of 300,000 kilometres per second, the distance it travels in one year is 9.5 trillion kilometres. Some stars in our galaxy are thousands of light years away, while other galaxies are billions of light years away.

The Big Bang

Most scientists today believe that the Universe started 13.8 billion years ago with an event known as the **Big Bang**. **Matter**, space and time all began at this moment. This idea is called the Big Bang Theory.

▼ *An artist's impression of how the Universe expanded from a single point following the Big Bang.*

THE FIRST INSTANT

The Universe began as a single point that was very hot and dense. Just a tiny fraction of a second after the Big Bang, the Universe had a temperature that, if written down in celsius, would be the number one followed by 32 zeros. From this moment on, the Universe grew at an incredible speed.

PARTICLES

Within seconds, the Universe had stretched out and begun to cool down. After about 100 seconds, particles such as electrons, protons and neutrons had started to form. These are the particles that make up **atoms**.

The history of the Universe

Since its beginning 13.8 billion years ago as a very hot and dense point, the Universe has gone through several key stages to become the vast structure we see today.

INSTANT INFLATION

Scientists think that a fraction of a second after the Big Bang, the Universe went through an incredible change when it expanded even faster than the speed of light. This period in the history of the Universe is known as inflation. During inflation, the Universe doubled in size almost 90 times.

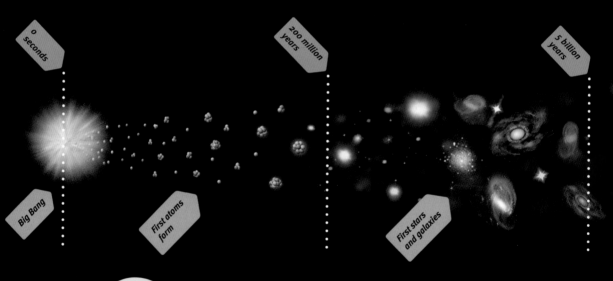

0 seconds

200 million years

5 billion years

Big Bang

First atoms form

First stars and galaxies

FIRST ATOMS

After about three minutes, the nuclei of simple **elements** such as hydrogen and helium formed out of the protons and neutrons that had appeared earlier (see page 9). The first atoms formed about 380,000 years later.

FIRST LIGHT

Once atoms formed, the first light also appeared. Known as 'cosmic microwave background radiation', it can still be detected today, though it has now cooled down to -270°C. This radiation tells astronomers a great deal about how the Universe came into being and the changes that happened when it was very young.

Scientists don't yet know what happened in the moments just after the Big Bang.

STARS AND GALAXIES

The first stars and galaxies started to form about 400 million years after the Big Bang, although it would be another 9 billion years before the Earth and Solar System appeared. Over the first few billion years, matter was pulled together by **gravity** to make huge numbers of galaxies, which in turn formed vast groups called clusters and superclusters. Other parts of the Universe had much less matter and very few galaxies. These almost empty parts of space are known as voids.

COSMIC YEAR

To help us understand how the Universe has changed since the Big Bang, imagine that the 13.8-billion-year history of the Universe is condensed down into just one year. Each month equals a little over a billion years. So, 1 January in this imaginary year would mark the Big Bang itself. The first stars would appear on 20 January and our Milky Way galaxy would be formed on 1 May.

9 billion years

10 billion years

Expansion of Universe accelerates

Solar System starts to form

Lif

The Sun and the Earth were formed in mid-September, while land plants first emerged on 19 December. The dinosaurs appeared on 25 December, but were wiped out on 29 December. In this model, the whole history of human civilization would fit into the last 20 seconds of the year.

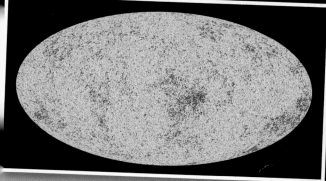

▲ *This is an image of cosmic microwave background radiation. The hotter areas, where superclusters of galaxies would later appear, are orange.*

Dark matter matters

When astronomers first studied how galaxies spin and move, they found that the amount of ordinary matter in these objects was not enough to explain their measurements. Scientists figured out that there must be additional matter present. The extra matter, which is invisible to our eyes and telescopes, is known as **dark matter**.

Scientists believe that a shell of dark matter surrounds the Milky Way.

UNIVERSE SECRETS

Dark matter does not emit any light, but it does have a pull due to gravity. Almost a quarter of the Universe is believed to be dark matter. Types of dark matter include dead stars, black holes, cold gas in space and particles much smaller than an atom.

Hot gas

Dark matter

STRAIGHT THROUGH YOU

Scientists believe that most dark matter is in the form of particles travelling through space. Billions of these particles pass through your body every second without you feeling anything.

SPOTTING IT

In this false-colour image of two colliding galaxy clusters, the pink areas show hot gas while the blue areas are dark matter. As dark matter doesn't interact with matter, it has travelled ahead of the gas, which has been slowed by the drag of the collision.

Dark energy

The Universe is mysterious. Ordinary matter makes up just 5 per cent of it. Another 24 per cent is dark matter. The other 71 per cent is even stranger than dark matter. Scientists have named this largest part dark energy, but no one really knows what it is. Today dark energy is one of the biggest mysteries in the Universe.

EXPANDING UNIVERSE

In the early 20th century, scientists believed the Universe was a fixed size. However, studies by the American astronomer Edwin Hubble in the 1920s proved that the Universe is still expanding.

▶ Edwin Hubble (1889–1953)

Dark energy is an unknown force that fills the Universe.

SLOWING DOWN?

In the 1990s, astronomers tried to measure how quickly the Universe has expanded since the Big Bang. They expected to find that it grew very quickly at the start, but that once galaxies formed, their gravity would slow down the speed of expansion.

▼ The study of the stars in this galaxy, NGC 4603, has shown that the expansion rate of the Universe is increasing.

Ordinary matter: 5 per cent

Dark matter: 24 per cent

Dark energy: 71 per cent

SPEEDING UP!

In fact, studies of faraway exploding stars have shown that the Universe is getting bigger at a faster rate. This is called an 'accelerating Universe'. To do this, a new force – dark energy – must be working against gravity, and must make up more than two thirds of the Universe.

How might it end?

Ever since scientists started to believe that the Universe began with the Big Bang, they have also wondered how it might end. Today we know that the galaxies are moving away from each other in a speedily expanding Universe, but what will happen billions of years in the future? There are three main ideas about the fate of the Universe. These are called the Big Crunch, the Big Freeze and the Big Rip.

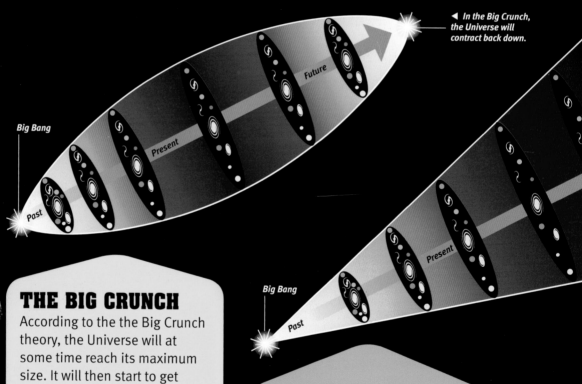

◄ In the Big Crunch, the Universe will contract back down.

THE BIG CRUNCH

According to the the Big Crunch theory, the Universe will at some time reach its maximum size. It will then start to get smaller, contracting in on itself. Eventually, all the matter in the Universe will collapse into the biggest-ever black hole.

THE BIG FREEZE

The Big Freeze theory suggests that the Universe will expand forever. As its matter is stretched farther apart, all of its heat will be spread out thinly across space. In the end nothing will remain warm in a dark and very cold Universe.

To decide which (if any) of the theories is correct, scientists are trying to measure how much matter of all types there is in the Universe. By studying far away galaxies, we hope to learn how they will change over time.

▶ This image taken by the Hubble Space Telescope shows some of the farthest and youngest galaxies ever detected in space.

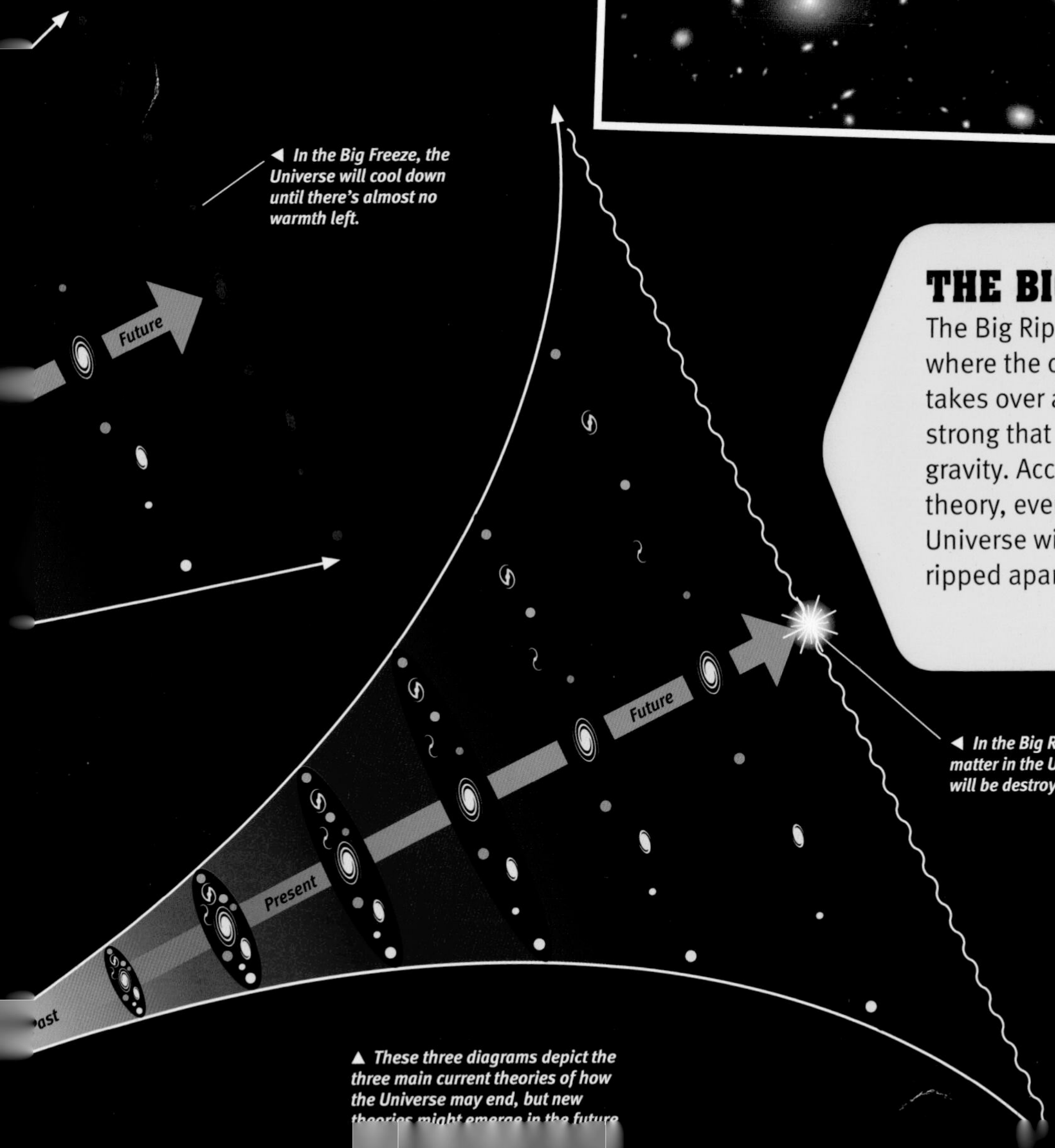

◀ In the Big Freeze, the Universe will cool down until there's almost no warmth left.

Future

THE BIG RIP

The Big Rip is a Universe where the dark energy takes over and becomes so strong that it overwhelms gravity. According to this theory, everything in the Universe will eventually be ripped apart.

◀ In the Big Rip, all matter in the Universe will be destroyed.

Future

Present

Past

▲ These three diagrams depict the three main current theories of how the Universe may end, but new theories might emerge in the future.

A Universe of galaxies

A galaxy is a huge collection of stars, gas and dust particles, all held together by gravity. We belong to a swirling galaxy called the Milky Way. Galaxies come in different shapes, sizes and ages, and can have between a million and a trillion stars in them.

Our galaxy, the Milky Way, measures about 120,000 light years across.

MESSIER'S LIST

Many of the brightest galaxies we know about today were first spotted in the 18th century by a French astronomer called Charles Messier. However, Messier did not know at the time what these 'fuzzy' objects were. He made a list of what he saw, and many galaxies still carry the names Messier gave them. Examples of galaxies from Messier's list include M31, M51 and M100.

◄ The influential French astronomer Charles Messier (1730–1817).

► A modern, close-up view of M51, one of Messier's fuzzy objects.

Trillions of stars
A galaxy can be home to more than a trillion stars (see above).

Billions of galaxies
Scientists believe there are more than 100 billion galaxies (see page 17).

CEPHEIDS

Until less than a century ago, scientists thought that our own Milky Way was the only galaxy in the Universe. In the late 1920s, Edwin Hubble studied some very bright stars called Cepheid variables that could be seen in the fuzzy objects in Messier's list. Hubble worked out that these fuzzy objects were millions of light years away. This meant that they must be other galaxies. Today astronomers estimate that there are at least 100 billion galaxies in the Universe.

THE FARTHEST OBJECTS

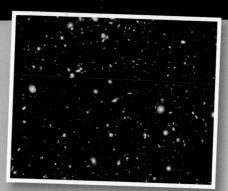

◀ *The light from these galaxies, some of the farthest and youngest in the Universe, has taken 13.2 billion light years to reach us.*

To understand how galaxies form, we have to look at the farthest objects in the Universe – which are also the youngest objects. This is because the farther away an object is, the longer its light takes to reach us. For instance, the nearest star to the Solar System, Proxima Centauri, is about four light years away, so we are seeing it as it was about four years ago.

The star RS Puppis, shown here, is a Cepheid variable – a type of star that brightens and dims regularly, and which can be used to measure distances in space.

▲ *The small galaxy in the bottom left is typical of galaxies in the early stages of the Universe.*

YOUNG GALAXIES

By looking at parts of the Universe that are more than 10 billion light years away, we can see the birth of new galaxies. The first galaxies formed just 200 million years after the Big Bang. These began as small, clumpy objects, but over millions of years, they built up into larger structures, such as our own spiral-shaped Milky Way.

Types of galaxy

There are three galaxy types: spirals, ellipticals and irregulars (see pages 18–19).

Our home

We inhabit a spiral galaxy called the Milky Way (see pages 20–21).

Local Group

Our galaxy is part of a group of galaxies (see pages 22–23).

Collisions

Sometimes galaxies crash into each other (see pages 22–23).

Types of galaxy

Galaxies come in a variety of shapes, sizes, colours and ages. A galaxy can be an enormous collection of more than a trillion stars, or a dwarf galaxy with just a million stars. Astronomers group galaxies according to their shapes. There are three main types of galaxy. They are called ellipticals, irregulars and spirals.

▼ *The edge of the elliptical galaxy known as M60 in the centre of this image overlaps with the spiral galaxy called NGC 4647 in the top right.*

ELLIPTICALS

Elliptical galaxies are shaped like an egg or a fuzzy oval football. The largest galaxies in the Universe are ellipticals. Some have more than a trillion stars and can stretch a million light years across, making them more than ten times the size of our galaxy! Some ellipticals become so enormous because they swallow up smaller galaxies around them.

ACTIVE GALAXIES

Astronomers sometimes label a galaxy according to how powerful it is. The most active galaxies contain quasars. These are very energetic central regions that are powered by black holes to produce huge amounts of light.

▼ NGC 1569 is an irregular galaxy located about 11 million light years from the Earth. Stars inside this galaxy are being formed very quickly – about 100 times faster than stars are being formed in our own galaxy.

IRREGULARS

As the name suggests, irregular galaxies have no shape or pattern. They are among the smallest galaxies. Their stars, gas and dust are spread out in all directions. Some astronomers think that irregular galaxies are the building blocks from which much larger galaxies formed.

SPIRALS

Resembling huge pinwheels, spirals are perhaps the most beautiful galaxies. They are flat discs of stars with a bright central bulge. The spiral arms wrap around the bulge as the whole galaxy turns around its centre. Spiral galaxies contain young and old stars. They also consist of huge amounts of gas and dust that are being used all the time to make new stars. The Milky Way is a spiral, and so is the galaxy known as M74, shown to the left.

Central bulge

Galactic arm

▲ Galaxy M74 may contain about 100 billion stars, which are arranged in a central bulge and two huge arms. It is located about 30 million light years from the Earth.

The Sun orbits around the centre of our galaxy at about 220 kilometres per second.

20

We live in a giant whirlpool-shaped galaxy called the Milky Way, which is made up of at least 100 billion stars. The number of stars in our galaxy is not fixed, since some stars are dying, while others are being born in cold gas clouds.

Spiral arm

Central bulge

Our Solar System

OUR HOME IN SPACE

Our galaxy is shaped like a thin disc, with spiral arms spreading out from the central bulge. We live on one of these arms, which contain the youngest stars. The Solar System is 27,000 light years away from the centre of the galaxy.

INTERSTELLAR MEDIUM

The Milky Way has lots of gas and dust in it, which lies in the space between stars. This is known as the interstellar medium. Almost 15 per cent of the matter we can see in telescopes in our galaxy is in the form of gas and dust. These are the regions where new stars are being made.

◄ The yellow spots in this image are huge clouds of gas and dust. These are areas of massive star formation.

BLACK HOLE HEART

There is an enormous amount of matter blocking our view of the centre of the galaxy. But by measuring powerful **X-rays** coming from the centre and the movement of stars near to it, astronomers have worked out that there is a supermassive black hole at the heart of the Milky Way. This black hole has a mass of about 4 billion Suns.

THE DARK HALO

Our galaxy is surrounded by a halo of matter. This sphere-like halo contains about 200 tightly packed groups of mostly old stars. These groups are called globular clusters, and each has between 100,000 and a million stars. Scientists think that more than half of the mass of the Milky Way is in the halo, but that it is invisible dark matter.

▶ A globular cluster of old stars in the halo of our galaxy.

MAPPING THE STARS

Since we live inside the Milky Way, we cannot simply take an image of it from above. Instead astronomers use telescopes to map out where the main stars and clumps of gas around us are. Using this information, and by looking at other galaxies, they have worked out the shape of our galaxy.

◀ The ALMA (Atacama Large Millimeter Array), a collection of 66 radio telescopes in Chile, has taken some very detailed images of the Milky Way.

The Local Group

Most galaxies are clumped together into groups. The Milky Way lies in a group called the Local Group. The Local Group is made up of about 30 galaxies, the largest two of which are the Milky Way and a spiral galaxy called Andromeda.

GALACTIC CRASH

Sometimes gravity can bring galaxies so close that they crash together. These galaxy collisions can take millions of years to happen, so we can't watch one from start to finish. Instead, astronomers use telescopes to take images of galaxies that are currently coming together, and in different stages of a collision. Lots of new stars are made when galaxies crash and clouds of gas are squeezed.

NGC 2207

IC 2163

▲ A large galaxy, NGC 2207, has drawn a smaller one, IC 2163, towards it, distorting its shape.

COLLISION COURSE

The Milky Way and the Andromeda galaxies are on a collision course. The two galaxies are about two million light years away, but are heading towards each other at a speed of 500,000 kilometres per hour. They will start to merge together about 4 billion years from now.

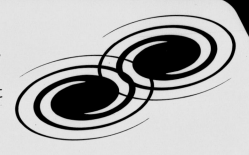

The Milky Way has grown by colliding with and absorbing other galaxies.

Our Local Group and about 100 other galaxy groups form a larger structure in space called the Virgo Supercluster. This is about 110 million light years across, and is one of millions of superclusters that make up the Universe.

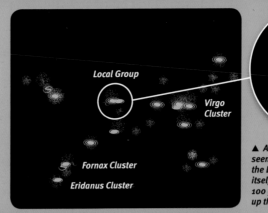

Local Group

Virgo Cluster

Fornax Cluster

Eridanus Cluster

Milky Way

Andromeda Galaxy

▲ As vast as our Milky Way seems, it's just one galaxy in the Local Group, which is itself just one of around 100 galaxy groups that make up the Virgo Supercluster.

GIANT GALAXY

Sometimes galaxies smashing together can create some very bizarre objects. One such example is the galaxy NGC 6872, located about 210 million light years from the Earth. One of the largest known spiral galaxies, the distance between its two arms is 500,000 light years, making it almost five times bigger than the Milky Way. Its great size is a result of it having collided with another galaxy called IC 4970 about 130 million years ago.

▼ NGC 6872's long, stretched-out shape was caused by its interaction with the smaller IC 4970 galaxy located above it.

CLUSTER CLASH

One of the biggest known collisions in the Universe takes place when two galaxy clusters collide. When this happens, the vast gravitational forces toss the galaxies around, producing very high energies and temperatures of up to 100 million°C in the space between galaxies.

▼ An artist's impression of a cluster clash, which can churn up extraordinarily hot gases.

Stars are not forever

One of the biggest breakthroughs of modern science has been the discovery that stars do not shine forever. They do, however, last a long time, with life cycles that are completed in millions or billions of years.

Our understanding of very young stars has been improved by using giant radio telescopes, such as this one.

◄ *This is the constellation of Orion, the Hunter.*

CONSTELLATIONS

In ancient times, people made patterns out of the brightest stars, often related to their myths. These made-up patterns are called constellations. Sailors once used them to navigate across the seas, and astronomers still work out positions of objects in the sky using constellations. Today we use 88 constellations to map out the sky, between the northern and southern hemispheres (the halves of the Earth divided by the equator).

Stellar nurseries
Stars form in clouds of gas and dust called

Nuclear fuelled
A star shines because of nuclear fusion reactions

GREAT BALLS OF FIRE

Stars are gigantic balls of burning gas, mostly made of hydrogen and helium. Our star, the Sun, has a diameter of about 1,390,000 kilometres, and its mass (its amount of matter) is so huge that if written down in kilograms it would be a 2 followed by 30 zeros. There are other stars in our galaxy that are 100 times larger than the Sun.

hot, burning surface of the star we know most about, our Sun.

THE LIFE OF A STAR

Stars are born in **nebulae** – dusty clouds of gas in space – and they change slowly over time. When stars can no longer generate the energy to shine, they change drastically and eventually die. How quickly a star changes and what happens to it at the end depends a lot on how massive it was when it was first made. Stars like our Sun are among the less massive stars and will last for about ten billion years. Other stars may be 20 to 100 times more massive than the Sun when they are born. These enormous stars lead very short lives of perhaps just a few million years. Massive stars end their lives by exploding in powerful events called **supernovae**.

▶ The Eagle Nebula is 7000 light years away and is a region of active star birth.

Lives of stars

Stars like our Sun become red giants at the end of their lives (see pages 30–31).

Blowouts

Supermassive stars end up exploding as supernovae (see page 33).

Born again

The matter from old stars can end up forming new ones (see page 34).

Blacked out

The most massive stars of all end up as black holes (see page 37).

In the 100 billion galaxies we can see, astronomers estimate that about 100 billion stars in total are being born every year. So where are they formed?

STAR CLOUDS

You need to bring together huge amounts of gas, mostly hydrogen, to make a star. In galaxies, this gas, along with dust particles, is found in enormous clouds called nebulae. The Orion Nebula in the constellation of Orion is an example of a star-making cloud. It lies about 1300 light years from the Earth and measures 40 light years across.

SQUEEZING STARS

Stars are made when the gas and dust in a giant nebula start to clump together. Gravity squeezes the matter, heating the gas. Over many years, the gas inside this clump reaches temperatures of 15 million°C. At these temperatures, huge amounts of energy can be generated by a reaction called **nuclear fusion**. When nuclear fusion begins, a star is born and it starts to shine brightly.

▲ This image shows young, hot stars forming in a galaxy some 13 million light years away.

▲ The clouds of gas and dust in the Orion Nebula are lit up by the huge amounts of energy from the newly born stars that are forming inside them.

Nuclear powered

The Sun and other stars are powered by nuclear fusion reactions in their cores. Nuclear fusion occurs when two or more nuclei of an element combine to make a heavier element. It takes place inside the Sun at a temperature of 15 million°C and at a pressure that is 250 billion times greater than that on the Earth's surface.

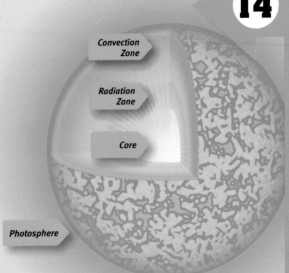

Convection Zone

Radiation Zone

Core

Photosphere

▲ Energy released by fusion in the Sun's core has to travel through different layers or zones before it reaches the surface, or photosphere, and is released into space.

▶ In nuclear fusion, the nuclei of two different types of hydrogen – deuterium and tritium – are squeezed together (or fused) to make helium, releasing enormous amounts of energy.

Deuterium nucleus

Helium nucleus

Fusion

Energy

Tritium nucleus

Neutron

GETTING HEAVY

In stars that are more massive than the Sun, other elements, apart from hydrogen, are fused to make energy. The temperature in the cores of these stars can be greater than one billion°C – hot enough to fuse helium into carbon. In even more massive stars, carbon can be fused to make oxygen, and oxygen fused to form silicon. In this manner, stars can fuse heavier and heavier elements by fusion reactions, until the core of a star is made of iron.

POWER CUT

As long as there is fuel in the core of a star for fusion reactions, there will be energy to keep the star going. In all stars, this fuel will eventually run out, and then the star will change. Sometimes this change can be dramatic and the star explodes!

To keep shining, the Sun converts 4 million tonnes of matter into energy every second.

Stellar evolution

The stages that a star goes through from birth to death are known as 'stellar evolution'. During this cycle the main things that change are the temperature, size and power of the star.

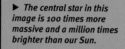

▶ *The central star in this image is 100 times more massive and a million times brighter than our Sun.*

◀ *The stellar life cycle begins in the Rosette Nebula as thousands of hot, young stars burst into life.*

BATTLE OF FORCES

During its life, a star is locked in a battle between two forces. Gravity is trying to crush the star and make it collapse. To stop this, gases inside the star have to be very hot and provide pressure to push back against gravity. When the crush of gravity and the outward push of the gases are equal, the star is stable. However, if the star's fuel runs out, the gases no longer provide the pressure. The star will collapse and begin to die out.

Most stars that can be seen with the naked eye are bigger than our Sun.

▼ *This artist's impression shows a young star (about a million years old), around which planets have begun to form out of a disc of gas and dust.*

Disc of gas and dust

Planet

Young star

STAR DETECTIVES

We cannot just stare at a star and watch it complete its very long life cycle. To understand how stars evolve, astronomers study lots of different stars at different stages of their lives, including ones that are newly born, shining brightly, beginning to die, or have already died. They look at these different objects and their properties to figure out how one must change into the other over the course of a stellar life.

ALIEN DETECTIVES

To understand how astronomers work out the life cycle of a star, imagine if an alien from another world visited and had just 24 hours to work out the life cycle of humans. One day is not long enough to see a person age from birth to death. Instead, the alien might visit a hospital to see babies being born, watch children playing in a school, see teenagers sitting in a park, and meet parents and grandparents. The alien could figure out that the baby becomes a child, and then a teenager, parent and grandparent, and so work out the whole human life cycle.

▼ *The Sagittarius Star Cloud contains millions of stars of all different ages.*

Life cycle of the Sun

About 5 billion years ago, a cloud of gas and dust began to collapse under gravity. The matter in the cloud was squeezed into a clump. The core of this clump became very hot, reaching 15 million°C when nuclear fusion reactions began. A new star was born.

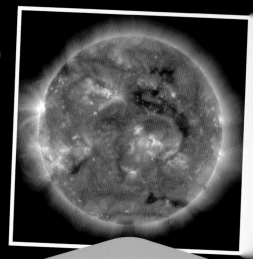

When the Sun becomes a red giant, it will have already lost 20 per cent of its mass.

HOW LONG LEFT?

The Sun has enough hydrogen fuel to continue nuclear reactions for about another 5 billion years. When all the hydrogen has been fused into helium, there will be no new energy to push against gravity. The Sun will then start to bloat outwards, turning into a red giant star more than 30 times larger than it is today. Mercury and Venus will be consumed beneath the red giant's outer layers. The Sun will almost reach the Earth, boiling off our oceans and **atmosphere** and melting the rocky surface.

A STABLE STAR

About 4.6 billion years old, the Sun is a stable star, shining through fusion reactions in its core. These reactions release light as gamma ray radiation (see page 72), which takes 100,000 years to travel through the interior. During this time, the gamma rays slowly lose energy. Eventually they emerge at the surface of the Sun as visible light and ultraviolet rays.

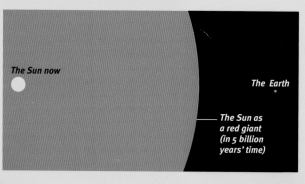

The Sun now

The Earth

The Sun as a red giant (in 5 billion years' time)

▲ Red giant stars in the Omega Centauri star cluster.

WHITE DWARF

After a few million years as a red giant, the outer layers of the Sun will be completely ejected into space. This stage of the life cycle is called a planetary nebula, and it signals the start of the Sun's death. The core left behind will be crushed by gravity into a very compact **body** about the size of the Earth, known as a white dwarf star. This is the final stage in the Sun's evolution. Over billions of years the white dwarf will give off all its heat to become a cold, dead star.

▼ *The dust and gas clouds of the planetary nebula NGC 3132 billow out from the compact white dwarf star at its centre.*

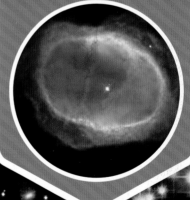

▲ *The appearance of this planetary nebula, known as the Helix Nebula, has led to it being given the nickname 'Eye of God'. It is about 700 light years away in the constellation of Aquarius.*

▲ *Old white dwarf stars shine in the globular cluster NGC 6397.*

Massive stars live fast

Some massive stars can have 100 times more matter than the Sun. They shine very brightly and powerfully, but they use up their fuel quickly, which means they have much shorter lives than the Sun.

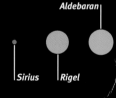

▼ Eta Carinae is an old, massive star, which is surrounded by clouds of material that blew off during a 19th-century explosion.

RED SUPERGIANTS

After their birth in a giant nebula, massive stars have a brief stage when they are stable against gravity and can fuse hydrogen to helium to make energy. But once this phase is over, these stars quickly bloat out to become supergiants. Betelgeuse in the constellation of Orion is a well-known bright, red supergiant, which has swelled up to almost a thousand times the size of the Sun.

Aldebaran

Betelgeuse

Antares

▶ Our Sun is dwarfed by the Universe's supergiant stars.

Our Sun | Sirius | Rigel

UNSTABLE STARS

As they age, massive stars become more unstable and start to shed their outer layers. The core of a supergiant star is more than 100 billion°C , and can fuse heavier elements, such as carbon and oxygen. Once the core is made of iron, however, all fuel has been used up. Now the star faces a violent death in a supernova explosion.

▲ The star Kappa Cassiopeiae is framed by a red ring, where the star's magnetic field interacts with the surrounding gas and dust.

Supernova explosions

The final phase in the life cycle of a massive star takes place when no more energy can be generated in its interior. The supergiant star now faces the crushing force of gravity.

◀ An artist's impression of a supernova blast in the night sky.

SHINING BRIGHTLY

An exploding supernova can have the brightness of more than 100 million Suns. In fact, a supernova can shine brighter than its entire galaxy. The leftover matter from the explosion is called a supernova remnant. This material contains all the matter that was in the star, including the chemical elements created in the fusion reactions. Elements heavier than iron, such as gold and silver, can also be forged during the supernova. The dead core of the star may become a **neutron star** or a black hole.

STAR EXPLOSION

Once all the star's fuel has gone, almost in an instant the gravitational force crushes the outer layers of the star. Within seconds, these layers smash violently into the densely packed core, and then rebound out with a shockwave. This is the supernova explosion. The shockwave drives away into space all the outer layers, ejecting them at speeds of up to 300,000 kilometres per hour. Astronomers observe many supernova explosions every year.

▼ The swirling gases and dust of the Veil Nebula are the remnants of a supernova that exploded between 5000 and 8000 years ago.

Astronomers estimate there are three supernovae in the Milky Way every year.

19

Cosmic recycling

Galaxies act as giant recycling plants for stars. Each galaxy has billions of stars at different stages in their lives. Some are just forming, some are burning brightly, and others are dying. The matter of dead stars will eventually be used to make new stars.

BIRTH AND LIFE

Cosmic recycling starts with the birth of new stars from giant nebulae of dust and gas. Nuclear reactions within the stars create new chemical elements until these stars themselves die, producing nebulae from which new stars form. By going around this cycle many times, the nebulae build up more and more heavier elements, such as carbon, silicon and oxygen.

Matter forms stars in nebula

Stars shinin brightly

Matter is redistributed

▶ In the Stellar 'Circle of Life', matter in galaxies is constantly being recycled.

Star exploding

Star ejecting mattter

THIRD-GENERATION STAR

After measuring the elements in our Sun, scientists think that it is a third-generation star. Heavier elements such as iron and gold are found in the Sun, and these can only be made inside supermassive stars. This means that the Sun was formed from a cloud of gas and dust that contained elements produced by a supernova. These elements allowed the formation of rocky planets in the Solar System, and also provided the chemical building blocks that allowed life to evolve on the Earth.

White dwarf tombstones

When the Sun becomes a white dwarf in about 5 billion years' time (see page 31), its mass will be about half what it is today. But gravity will have crushed this matter into a tightly packed ball about the size of the Earth. A piece of white dwarf material the size of a sugar cube would weigh a tonne on the Earth.

CRYSTAL STARS

The cores of many white dwarf stars are made of carbon. As the stars cool down over millions of years, the carbon becomes crystallized as diamond. This means that the remains of many Sun-like stars are gigantic uncut diamonds hanging in space.

The gravity of a white dwarf star is 350,000 times greater than that of the Earth.

SIRIUS B

Sirius, the brightest star in the night sky, is in fact a star system made up of three stars, about 8.6 light years away. One of these stars, Sirius B, was among the first white dwarfs to be discovered. Astronomers think that Sirius B was born around 60 million years ago with a mass about five times that of the Sun. Over time the star shed matter into space and died out as a white dwarf with a mass down to about that of the Sun.

Sirius B

Sirius A

▲ Sirius B, the blue star in this image, is much less bright than Sirius A.

Neutron stars and pulsars

Neutron stars are dead stars that are packed so tightly they would fit inside a city. These objects are born out of supernovae. The core of the star that is left after the explosion is crushed so forcefully that it is made of particles called neutrons.

▼ *The Crab Nebula was created by a supernova in the year 1054. At its centre is a neutron star, measuring 20 km across and spinning at 30 times a second.*

GETTING HEAVY

A typical neutron star has a pull of gravity that is 2 billion times stronger than what we feel on the surface of the Earth. A piece of neutron star the size of a sugar cube would weigh a billion tonnes on the Earth.

SPINNING FAST

When a star is crushed down in a supernova explosion, it starts to spin very fast – up to 40,000 times a minute. It also develops a strong magnetic field and beams out pulses of radiation. These pulses are detected by radio telescopes on the Earth, which led astronomers to name these objects pulsars. All pulsars are neutron stars.

▲ *Illustration of a neutron star emitting pulses of extremely high-energy particles.*

More than 600 pulsars have been discovered, and there may be another 100,000 out there.

Black holes

The most massive stars end up as black holes – regions of space where matter has been squeezed in on itself. The space around a black hole is very warped, and gravity is so powerful that nothing, not even light, can escape.

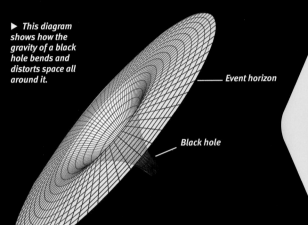

▶ This diagram shows how the gravity of a black hole bends and distorts space all around it.

Event horizon

Black hole

NO ESCAPE!

Most black holes are just a few times the Sun's mass, but some are the remnants of stars born with many times its mass. In the instant of a supernova, the core collapses and reaches 100 billion°C. Nothing can stop the squeeze of gravity now.

X-rays

Black hole

EVENT HORIZON

Thankfully, black holes are not cosmic vacuum cleaners sweeping up everything in the Universe. You'd have to get very close to a black hole to be trapped by it. The edge of a black hole is called the Event Horizon. Anything crossing this is lost forever. If an astronaut fell into a black hole he or she would be stretched like a piece of spaghetti, and then completely pulled apart by the gravity.

▲ An artist's impression of a disc of matter being slowly sucked into a black hole. Vast amounts of X-rays emerge from the disc.

Huge black holes in galaxy centres can be millions of times as massive as the Sun.

Exploring the Solar System

Our understanding of the Solar System has improved greatly over the past 50 years. Today, Solar System exploration is mainly carried out on missions using robotic spacecraft and **landers**.

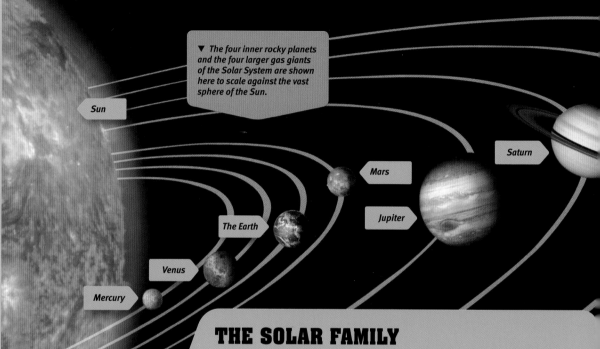

▼ *The four inner rocky planets and the four larger gas giants of the Solar System are shown here to scale against the vast sphere of the Sun.*

Sun

Saturn

Mars

Jupiter

The Earth

Venus

Mercury

THE SOLAR FAMILY

The Solar System is made up of eight planets, more than 170 moons, several dwarf planets, millions of rocky asteroids and billions of icy comets. However, the Sun makes up almost 98 per cent of the mass of the Solar System. Small, rocky planets were made close to the Sun, where temperatures are very high. In the colder outer region, much larger planets were formed which had strong gravities that could trap lots of gas and build up huge atmospheres.

Mercury
Mercury is the Solar System's most cratered planet (see page 42).

Venus
Its thick atmosphere makes Venus the hottest planet (see page 43).

Earth
The Earth is the only planet known to support life (see page 44).

Mars
Several robotic rovers have explored Mars's surface (see page 45).

The Solar System formed out of a giant cloud of gas and dust 4.6 billion years ago. The gas collapsed under the weight of its own gravity and started spinning. At the centre, our Sun began to grow and the leftover material formed a plate-like disc around it. In this disc, particles clumped together to build moons and planets.

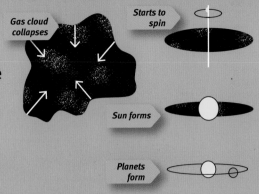

Gas cloud collapses

Starts to spin

Sun forms

Planets form

DWARF PLANETS

Our Solar System is also home to several dwarf planets, which are much smaller than planets. There are currently five dwarf planets: Ceres, Pluto, Eris, Makemake and Haumea, but scientists believe there may be dozens more.

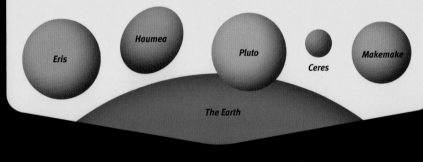

Eris

Haumea

Pluto

Ceres

Makemake

The Earth

Neptune

Uranus

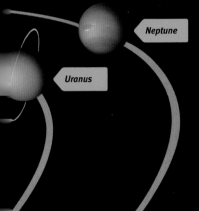

▲ The irregularly shaped asteroid 243 Ida has its own tiny moon, Dactyl.

► Halley's Comet visits the inner Solar System every 76 years.

ASTEROIDS AND COMETS

There are billions of small objects in the Solar System. These include asteroids made of rock and metal, most of which are found in a doughnut-shaped region between Mars and Jupiter called the Asteroid Belt. Vast numbers of comets are found in a giant area known as the Oort Cloud. The Oort Cloud is like a bubble of leftover material around the rest of the Solar System.

Planet facts

MARS

Diameter (km): 6792

Mass (compared to the Earth): 0.107

Gravity (compared to the Earth): 0.38

The eight planets range from tiny Mercury, which doesn't have a moon, to giant Jupiter, which has **67** of them.

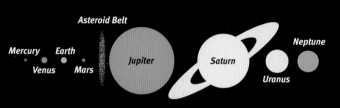

Asteroid Belt

Mercury Earth

Venus Mars

Jupiter

Saturn

Uranus

Neptune

▲ *If the distances between the planets were shown to scale, this book would have to be hundreds of metres long.*

MERCURY

Diameter (km): 4879

Mass (compared to the Earth): 0.055

Gravity (compared to the Earth): 0.38

Average distance from Sun (million km): 57.9

Rotation period (hours): 1407.6

Orbital period (in Earth years): 0.24

Number of known moons: 0

Atmosphere composition: None

VENUS

Diameter (km): 12,104

Mass (compared to the Earth): 0.815

Gravity (compared to the Earth): 0.9

Average distance from Sun (million km): 108.2

Rotation period (hours): 5832.5

Orbital period (in Earth years): 0.62

Number of known moons: 0

Atmosphere composition: Carbon dioxide (very thick)

EARTH

Diameter (km): 12,756

Mass (compared to the Earth): 1

Gravity (compared to the Earth): 1

Average distance from Sun (million km): 149.6

Rotation period (hours): 23.9

Orbital period (in Earth years): 1

Number of known moons: 1

Atmosphere composition: Nitrogen, oxygen (thick)

Average distance from Sun (million km): 227.9

Rotation period (hours): 24.6

Orbital period (in Earth years): 1.88

Number of known moons: 2

Atmosphere composition: Carbon dioxide (thin)

JUPITER

Diameter (km): 142,984

Mass (compared to the Earth): 318

Gravity (compared to the Earth): 2.64

Average distance from Sun (million km): 778.6

Rotation period (hours): 9.9

Orbital period (in Earth years): 11.9

Number of known moons: 67

Atmosphere composition: Hydrogen, helium, methane (very thick)

SATURN

Diameter (km): 120,536

Mass (compared to the Earth): 95

Gravity (compared to the Earth): 0.93

Average distance from Sun (million km): 1434

Rotation period (hours): 10.7

Orbital period (in Earth years): 29.5

Number of known moons: 62

Atmosphere composition: Hydrogen, helium, methane (very thick)

NEPTUNE

Diameter (km): 49,528

Mass (compared to the Earth): 17

Gravity (compared to the Earth): 1.12

Average distance from Sun (million km): 4495

Rotation period (hours): 16.1

Orbital period (in Earth years): 164.8

Number of known moons: 14

Atmosphere composition: Hydrogen, helium, methane (very thick)

URANUS

Diameter (km): 51,118

Mass (compared to the Earth): 15

Gravity (compared to the Earth): 0.89

Average distance from Sun (million km): 2873

Rotation period (hours): 17.2

Orbital period (in Earth years): 84.0

Number of known moons: 27

Atmosphere composition: Hydrogen, helium, methane (very thick)

Messenger to Mercury

Mercury is difficult to observe and explore because it is so close to the Sun. The daytime temperature can rise to a scorching 450°C, but as there is no atmosphere, the nights can be extremely cold, sinking below -180°C. The planet's surface is covered in craters made by comet and asteroid crashes.

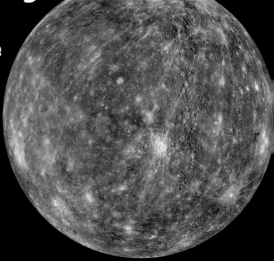

▼ A false-colour image of Mercury taken by Messenger, highlighting the different rocks that make up the planet's surface.

EXPLORING MERCURY

Launched on 3 August 2004, NASA's *Messenger* was the first spacecraft to orbit Mercury. From March 2011 onwards, it spent four years mapping the surface of Mercury. It closely studied freezing craters at the north pole containing water ice, which was probably brought there by comets and asteroids crashing into the planet millions of years ago.

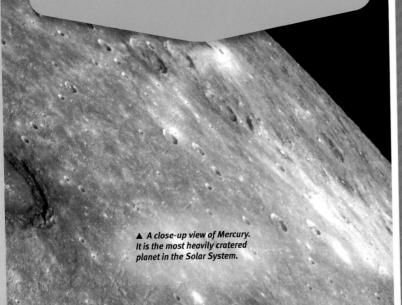

▲ A close-up view of Mercury. It is the most heavily cratered planet in the Solar System.

CRASH LANDING

By 2015, *Messenger* had run out of fuel and reached the end of its mission. So, on 30 April 2015, scientists crashed the spacecraft onto Mercury. It hit the planet's surface at a speed of 14,080 kilometres per hour, resulting in a 16-metre-wide hole in the ground.

Venus Express

Sometimes called the Earth's twin, Venus is about the same size as our planet, and is made of similar rocky material. But its thick, deadly carbon dioxide atmosphere is very different, and acts like a blanket that heats the planet's surface to a roasting 465°C.

▲ *An artist's impression of the* Venus Express *spacecraft in orbit around Venus.*

STILL ACTIVE?

Much of Venus's surface is covered in volcanoes. Until recently, scientists thought these were extinct. However, *Venus Express* discovered ozone and a mysterious layer of sulphur dioxide in the planet's atmosphere, which suggests that some of the volcanoes might still be active and erupting today.

MISSION TO VENUS

The European Space Agency (ESA) launched *Venus Express* in November 2005. It arrived at the planet in April 2006. It spent eight years studying the planet's atmosphere, sending back information to scientists.

▲ *Venus has more ancient volcanoes than any other planet in the Solar System.*

Our Earth

Formed 4.6 billion years ago, the Earth is the third planet from the Sun and, at 12,756 km across, the fifth largest planet in the Solar System. Its distance from the Sun means that it is not too hot, nor too cold, but just the right temperature for life to exist.

◀ *The blue of the oceans and the swirling white patterns of clouds led astronauts to describe the Earth as a 'blue marble' floating in space.*

◀ *Liquid water makes the Earth the only planet in the Solar System known to have life.*

WATER WORLD

The Earth is the only body in the Solar System that has liquid water permanently on its surface. Almost 71 per cent of our planet is covered by water; it is mostly in the oceans, but a small amount is locked up in the ice sheets that cover the polar regions.

CHANGING FEATURES

The Earth has volcanoes that erupt and continents that move to make mountains and create earthquakes. Our planet is also wrapped in an atmosphere made up of 78 per cent nitrogen and 21 per cent oxygen, which acts like a protective blanket around it. Nowhere else in the Solar System has an atmosphere that is so rich in oxygen.

▼ *Erupting volcanoes pour liquid rock out onto the surface and throw huge amounts of gas and dust into the Earth's atmosphere.*

The Earth's spin is slowing down – in 140 million years, a day will be 25 hours.

ROBOTS

Since 1997, the exploration of Mars has been led by robot vehicles travelling around the planet's surface. The unmanned **rovers** have carried lots of scientific equipment, including high-definition cameras, scoops to collect samples, and even lasers and drills to break up rocks and see what they are made from.

Roving on Mars

More spacecraft missions have been sent to Mars than to any other planet. Mars is a small, rocky planet. Like the Earth, it has seasons and a 24-hour day. However, temperatures rarely rise above freezing, and the atmosphere is very thin and has almost no oxygen.

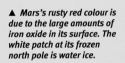

▲ Mars's rusty red colour is due to the large amounts of iron oxide in its surface. The white patch at its frozen north pole is water ice.

Opportunity has spent more than 3000 days on Mars and travelled over 40 km.

▲ Opportunity was one of a pair of rovers that landed on Mars in 2004.

GEOGRAPHY

Mars has some of the most extraordinary geography in the Solar System. It has the largest known volcano, *Olympus Mons*, which is 17 km high and 600 km wide, as well as the largest canyon: the *Valles Marineris,* which is 4000 km long and up to 7 km deep.

Asteroids up close

Asteroids are small rocky bodies. Millions of them lie in a region between Mars and Jupiter known as the Asteroid Belt. Some are made of rock, while others also contain metals, such as nickel and iron.

ASTEROID BELT

Asteroids are mostly the leftovers of material that formed the inner planets. Two of the largest bodies in the Asteroid Belt are Vesta and Ceres. Vesta is 525 kilometres wide, while Ceres measures 950 kilometres across. In September 2007, NASA launched the *Dawn* mission to explore these two objects in the Asteroid Belt.

▲ *Vesta, the brightest asteroid in the night sky, was discovered in 1807 by the German astronomer Heinrich Wilhelm Olbers.*

ASTEROID MISSION

Dawn arrived at Ceres in 2015, having first orbited Vesta in 2011. This mission sent back lots of data about the shape, size and structure of the asteroids, including information about their composition and magnetism.

▲ *The appearance of these strange bright spots inside craters on Ceres led many scientists to think that there might be water ice on the asteroid.*

King Jupiter

At nearly 143,000 kilometres across, Jupiter is the largest planet in the Solar System. A vast ball of gases surrounding a small rocky core, it has powerful winds, constant lightning strikes and a huge storm called the Great Red Spot. This has been raging for more than 300 years and is about twice the width of the Earth.

Io

Europa

▲ This image of Jupiter shows two of its largest moons, Io (passing in front of the Great Red Spot) and Europa.

Jupiter is so large that more than 1320 Earths could fit inside it.

EXPLORING A GIANT

The unmanned spacecraft *Galileo* arrived at Jupiter in December 1995 and spent eight years orbiting the planet. *Galileo* beamed back hundreds of fantastic images of the planet and its moons, and made lots of new measurements of the composition and magnetic field of Jupiter. On 21 September 2003, the *Galileo* mission ended when scientists deliberately plunged the spacecraft into the atmosphere of Jupiter, where it burnt up.

▼ Jupiter's moon Europa is covered by a thick layer of ice. The Galileo spacecraft found evidence that layers of salty water lie beneath this ice.

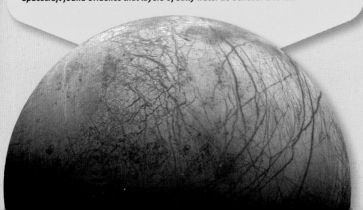

KING OF THE PLANETS

Jupiter has 67 known moons, the largest of which are Io, Europa, Callisto and Ganymede. Jupiter also has a thin set of dark rings, mostly made up of smoke-sized particles and dust.

The mysteries of Saturn

Saturn is a wonder of the Solar System. It is almost 120,000 kilometres across, making it the second-largest planet. It also has spectacular rings and is host to Titan, the only moon with a planet-like atmosphere.

Saturn's rings are 280,000 km from edge to edge, but only 10 metres thick.

RING SYSTEM

Saturn's rings were first noticed by the Italian astronomer Galileo Gallilei in 1610, using an early telescope. He wasn't sure what they were and described the planet as having two 'ears'. A few decades later, Dutch scientist Christiaan Huygens, using a more powerful telescope, saw what he thought was a ring surrounding the planet. In 1675, another Italian, Giovanni Cassini, found that the ring was actually made up of several rings.

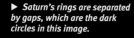
▶ Saturn's rings are separated by gaps, which are the dark circles in this image.

EXPLORING SATURN

Launched by NASA and the European Space Agency (ESA), *Cassini* has spent the last decade orbiting Saturn, flying through the rings and exploring its moons. It has beamed back thousands of images and used its many instruments to study the planet's atmosphere and magnetic field.

ATMOSPHERE

Saturn has a thick atmosphere of hydrogen and helium. Powerful storms rage on Saturn, with winds blowing at 1800 kilometres per hour near the equator. Lightning storms on Saturn can last for six months, firing bolts that are 10,000 times more powerful than those seen on the Earth.

RING PARTICLES

Cassini sent back many high-resolution images of Saturn's rings. There are more than 30 rings, and they are made from billions of lumps of rock and ice. These lumps range in size from particles the size of sugar grains to boulders as big as a house.

▲ *Saturn's rings appear to glow brightly in this image taken by Cassini looking back towards the Sun.*

◄ Cassini *was launched in October 1997 and took nearly seven years to reach Saturn, arriving in June 2004.*

▲ *Huygens used parachutes to slow its fall through Titan's thick atmosphere of nitrogen gas.*

TITAN PROBE

Cassini also carried a smaller craft called the *Huygens* **probe**, named after the Dutch astronomer. On 14 January 2005, *Huygens* successfully landed on Titan. Titan's surface is a very strange place, with lakes of liquid methane and oily riverbeds (see page 51).

49

Other ring systems

Although they are smaller and harder to see, the other three giant gas planets – Jupiter, Uranus and Neptune – have rings made up of swarms of icy particles.

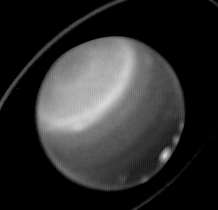

▲ An artist's impression of Jupiter's faint rings.

◄ A false-colour image of Uranus's ring system.

RING FORMATION

Most of the rings surrounding the gas giants probably formed at the same time as the planets. However, some of them could be material from moons torn apart by the gravity of the planets. Each ring system is made up of several separate rings with gaps made by the paths of the planet's moons.

NEW RINGS

Jupiter's rings were discovered in 1979 when the *Voyager 1* space probe flew past the planet. The giant planet has four main rings, which are very faint and dark because they are made mainly of dust. Uranus's rings are thought to be just 600 million years old. There are 13 of them, each a few kilometres wide and made up of faint bodies. Six rings have been discovered around Neptune, which are also very dark and difficult to observe. The rings were first spotted in 1989 when *Voyager 2* flew past Neptune.

▼ Neptune's faint rings captured by the *Voyager 2* spacecraft during its flyby.

Titan touchdown

▲ Here, Cassini has photographed Titan orbiting in front of Saturn.

The largest of Saturn's 62 known moons, Titan is the second-largest moon in the Solar System and the only one with a thick atmosphere and clouds of its own. Titan may be similar to how the Earth was billions of years ago when life first started.

With methane and ethane instead of water, Titan's longest river is 320 km long.

BELOW THE CLOUDS

The atmosphere of Titan is made up mostly of nitrogen gas and is so thick that it hides the surface. To find out more about the moon, scientists dropped the *Huygens* probe onto its surface in 2005 (see page 49). This is the first time we placed a lander on a moon other than our own. The probe's batteries lasted just over an hour, and it beamed back images and data. Scientists are planning future missions to Titan, including perhaps landing a floating probe on one of the moon's lakes.

▼ After its descent through Titan's atmosphere, Huygens came to rest on an area of damp, sand-like material surrounded by small pebbles.

▲ Titan's thick atmosphere gives the moon the appearance of a fuzzy brown ball.

STRANGE WORLD

The temperature on Titan is so cold that the natural gas we use on the Earth as fuel becomes an oily liquid on Titan, which runs into rivers and lakes on the surface. Strong winds blow there to make dunes of oily sand. Scientists think there may also be volcanoes, which erupt water ice rather than lava.

Rolling Uranus

All planets turn on a vertical axis like spinning tops, except Uranus, which spins on its side. Scientists think this is because a massive Earth-sized object crashed into Uranus billions of years ago and knocked it over.

▲ One of the first close-up views of Uranus taken by Voyager 2 in 1986.

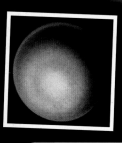

◄ This computer-enhanced image emphasizes Uranus's hazy upper atmosphere.

GASSY GIANT

The atmosphere of Uranus is mainly made up of hydrogen and helium, with a small amount of methane. The methane traps red light and scatters blue light, which is why the planet appears blue. Although we don't know for sure what Uranus's interior is like, scientists think that there is a slushy mixture of icy water, ammonia and methane that extends thousands of kilometres. The central part of the planet is probably a small rocky core.

SHAKESPEARE'S MOONS

Uranus's moons are unique in that all 27 are named after characters in the works of the playwright William Shakespeare. The largest moons, Oberon and Titania, were discovered by British astronomer William Herschel in 1787. Another, called Miranda, has giant canyons that are 12 times deeper than the Grand Canyon in the USA.

◄ Uranus's fifth largest moon, Miranda, is covered in canyons, valleys and craters.

Blue Neptune

Neptune is an almost identical twin to Uranus, with an atmosphere of hydrogen, helium and methane, but with a deeper blue colour. It probably has an interior of ices and a rocky core.

◄ It is methane that gives Neptune its deep blue colour. The Great Dark Spot is in the centre of this image.

WINDY PLANET

Neptune has the fastest winds in the Solar System. Wind speeds of up to 2400 kilometres per hour have been recorded in the storms of its upper atmosphere. The planet also has distinct cloud patterns, with bright methane clouds forming in the highest layers of its atmosphere, and water ice, hydrogen sulphide and ammonia clouds occurring in the deeper layers. Neptune's most distinctive feature is a giant 1280-kilometre-wide storm known as the Great Dark Spot.

► Winds in Neptune's upper atmosphere form long white clouds.

NEPTUNE'S MOONS

Triton is the largest of Neptune's 14 moons. It is possibly the only moon in the Solar System that orbits in a direction opposite to the rotation of the planet itself. In 1989, *Voyager 2* made a stunning discovery – there are active volcanoes on Triton's surface. Geyser-like volcanic vents are spewing out water ice and gases up to heights of 8 kilometres into space.

◄ A close-up image of the Great Dark Spot. It has come and gone several times since it was first spotted in 1989, although scientists are not sure why.

New Horizons at Pluto

Pluto is a dwarf planet that orbits in the outer Solar System. In July 2015, NASA's *New Horizons* spacecraft made the first ever flyby of Pluto. Having blasted off in January 2006, *New Horizons* travelled more than 4.8 billion kilometres to zoom just 12,500 kilometres above Pluto's surface.

Pluto is just 2400 kilometres across, making it smaller than the Earth's Moon.

▲ *Charon is the largest moon orbiting Pluto.*

▲ *Having passed Pluto, New Horizons is heading towards a tiny, frozen body deep in the outer Solar System called 2014 MU69. It is expected to reach this strange world in January 2019.*

PLUTO'S MOONS

New Horizons sent back the first close-up views of Pluto's five moons. Scientists think Charon may have ice volcanoes. The other moons are between 7 kilometres and 50 kilometres wide and are all strangely shaped. For example, Nix is oval and wobbles and tilts as it orbits Pluto.

RIVERS, CLIFFS AND VALLEYS

The images sent by *New Horizons* showed craters formed by the impact of bodies from space. It also spotted cliffs and valleys that may have been formed by the action of nitrogen ice on the surface and other processes. Instruments detected that Pluto has a thin atmosphere of nitrogen, methane and carbon dioxide.

Comet swarms

Comets are spectacular visitors in our night skies. They are small bodies, just a few kilometres across, made of rock and dirty snow. Comets store lots of water ice, and some scientists think they delivered water to the Earth when they hit our planet billions of years ago. The water carried by comets may have helped to fill our oceans.

▼ This image of Comet Hale Bopp shows the tail of gas and dust streaming out behind. Comet tails can measure 10 million kilometres long.

OORT CLOUD

Home to billions of icy bodies left over from when the Solar System formed, the Oort Cloud lies between 6500 and 13,000 billion kilometres from the Sun. Sometimes these icy bodies bump into each other, sending one towards the Sun. As it gets closer, it heats up, turning into a comet.

Oort Cloud

Sun

COMET TAILS

As a comet glides nearer to the Sun, the Sun's energy warms the comet's ice, causing it to boil off and form a tail. This is when a comet can become a fantastic sight in the night sky. Eventually, the comet will swing around the Sun on a huge curved path and head back into deep space and the cold region of the Oort Cloud.

The leftovers of comet tails create meteor showers in our night skies.

Exoplanets

There may be 2 billion habitable planets orbiting Sun-like stars in our galaxy.

In the past 20 years, technological advances have allowed astronomers to discover planets in our galaxy orbiting stars other than our own. Planets that lie beyond our Solar System are called **exoplanets**, and more than 1700 have been found. Scientists estimate that of the 200 billion stars in the Milky Way, more than 20 billion could have planetary systems.

DIFFICULT TO FIND

A star outshines its planets by between a million and a billion times. This means that it is very difficult to find an exoplanet simply by pointing a telescope at a star and taking an image. Astronomers have instead worked out several methods and use powerful telescopes to look for signals that indicate whether planets are orbiting distant stars.

WOBBLING STARS

The gravity of a planet makes its star wobble. For example, the Sun wobbles slightly due to the pull of Jupiter's gravity. The light from a wobbling star shifts slightly towards more blue or red wavelengths. Astronomers can detect these shifts to learn about the mass of the exoplanet. This is known as the radial velocity method.

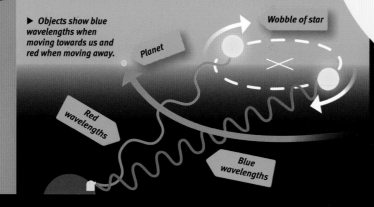

▶ Objects show blue wavelengths when moving towards us and red when moving away.

Planet

Wobble of star

Red wavelengths

Blue wavelengths

New worlds
Scientists have found hundreds of exoplanets (see above).

Push and pull
Large exoplanets cause their star to wobble slightly (see above).

Faint difference
Exoplanets cause their star to dim slightly as they pass in front (see page 57).

Planet spotting
The *Kepler* space telescope is on the lookout for exoplanets (see page 57).

DIMMING THE LIGHT

The radial velocity method works best for detecting large planets. A method called transiting is used to find smaller planets. When a planet passes across the face of a star, the starlight we see can be slightly dimmed. This mini-eclipse is called a transit. By carefully studying the brightness changes of stars during these transits, it is possible to detect less massive, Earth-like planets.

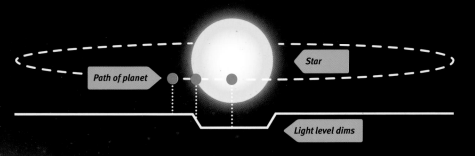

Path of planet

Star

Light level dims

◀ As an exoplanet travels in front of its star, it causes the star's light to dim very slightly. Astronomers can use this information to calculate the size of the exoplanet.

KEPLER TELESCOPE

Since 2009, the *Kepler* space observatory, a very sensitive telescope, has been measuring the brightness changes in more than 100,000 stars. To discover Earth-like planets, *Kepler* will need to detect a drop in brightness of just one hundredth of a per cent. That's like seeing a car's headlight dim when a fly moves in front of it.

◀ Illustration of two rocky planets orbiting in front of a star in a planet system discovered by Kepler.

◀ Kepler has discovered more than 1000 exoplanets so far.

Big heat
Gas giants orbiting near their star are known as hot Jupiters (see page 58).

Earth plus
Large Earth-like exoplanets are known as super-Earths (see page 59).

A new home?
Scientist are looking for Earth-like planets that could support life (see page 60).

Just right
For life to exist, an exoplanet must be in the 'Goldilocks Zone' (see page 61).

Hot Jupiters

One of the big surprises of exoplanet studies has been the discovery of gas giants orbiting very close to their stars. In many cases these giant planets are similar to Jupiter, but orbit much closer than Mercury does to our Sun. These planets, called 'hot Jupiters', go round their star every two to three days.

▼ *An artist's impression of the exoplanet HD 189733b where, scientists believe, winds can reach up to 9600 kilometres per hour, driven by the power of the nearby star.*

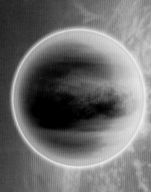

HOT PLANET

The exoplanet HD 189733b is 63 light years away and orbits its star 13 times closer than Mercury orbits the Sun. Its temperature can get as high as 925°C. Being so close to its star, HD 189733b is believed by scientists to be boiling away, losing almost 600 million kilograms of mass every second.

PLANET PUZZLE

Hot Jupiters are mysterious because there are no giant gas planets in the inner regions of our own Solar System. One theory is that the hot Jupiters did form far from the star, but then got pulled in as the system of planets settled down. Their discovery shows that there may be very different types of planet systems in our galaxy.

▲ *An artist's impression of an Earth-like moon (left) orbiting a Saturn-like planet. Many exoplanets probably have exomoons.*

The surface temperatures of hot Jupiters are so high they can melt silver.

A super-Earth is an exoplanet with more mass than the Earth, but less than a giant gas planet. A typical super-Earth could be made of rock and metal, and may have oceans or very thick atmospheres.

Molten surface

Cooling surface

SCORCHED EARTH

A super-Earth called 55 Cancri e has a diameter about twice that of the Earth and orbits extremely close to its star, resulting in scorching temperatures of about 2120°C. Being more massive, they also have stronger gravity, which may make any oceans and lakes on these planets much shallower than we have on the Earth.

▲ Scientists think that the side of 55 Cancri e that faces the Sun may become molten, before cooling as it turns away.

LAVA PLANET

Astronomers have found that a star called HD 219134, which lies 21 light years away, has a planet system of three super-Earths. One of these is 1.6 times larger in diameter and four times greater in mass than the Earth, and has a temperature of 430°C.

▲ The planet HD 219134b is the nearest exoplanet to the Earth yet found.

The super-Earth planet GJ 1214b may have water vapour in its atmosphere.

41

Hunting new Earths

One of the major goals of modern astronomers is to discover Earth-like planets. This means searching for worlds that are small and rocky, that orbit a middle-aged star which should continue to produce light and warmth for several billion years, and that could possibly have liquid water on their surface.

KEPLER-425b

One of the most Earth-like planets discovered so far, Kepler-425b was spotted in July 2015 by NASA's *Kepler* space observatory (see page 57). The exoplanet is about 1400 light years away from our Solar System in the constellation of Cygnus. It is orbiting a star that is almost the same temperature and size as the Sun. A year on Kepler-425b lasts 385 days, which means it must orbit its star at about the same distance as the Earth is from the Sun.

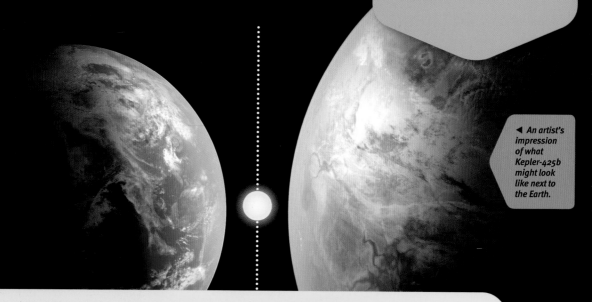

◀ *An artist's impression of what Kepler-425b might look like next to the Earth.*

OLDER COUSIN

Astronomers think that Kepler-425b may have an atmosphere, weather systems and even active volcanoes. They also estimate that Kepler-425b's star is 1.5 billion years older than the Sun, so life would have had more time to evolve. However, no one is sure whether Kepler-425b is habitable.

Keppler-22b Keppler-69c Keppler-425b Keppler-62f Keppler-186f Earth

◀ *The sizes of some of the most Earth-like exoplanets.*

Goldilocks planets

All living things on the Earth need water to survive, so astronomers are looking for exoplanets that are the right temperature for oceans and lakes of liquid water to exist. For this to happen, the exoplanets need to be the right distance from their stars so that they are neither too hot nor too cold – just like the porridge in the Goldilocks fairytale.

WATER WORLD

The Earth-like planet Kepler-442b is 1100 light years away, and it orbits its star in about 112 days. This star is much smaller and cooler than the Sun. Scientists believe it is very likely that Kepler-442b lies in the right region from its star for it to be a Goldilocks planet with liquid water on its surface.

JUST RIGHT

Finding Earth-like Goldilocks planets elsewhere in our galaxy is a very important part of NASA's *Kepler* mission. As well as being at the right temperature, these small, rocky exoplanets need to have thick atmospheres with high enough pressure to allow liquid water to stay on their surface.

▶ Kepler-62e, a possible Goldilocks planet, compared to the Earth.

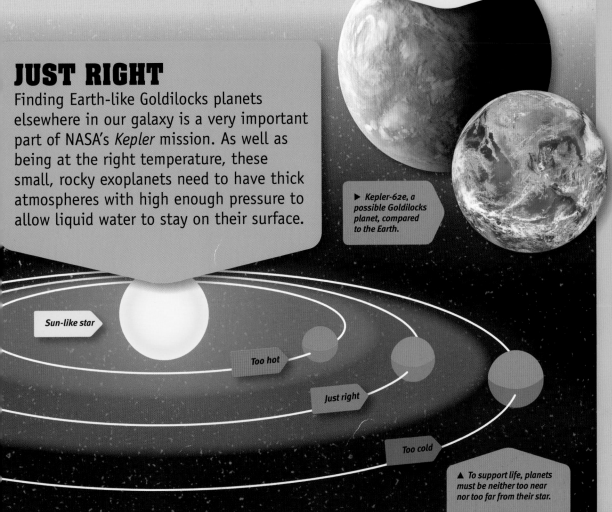

Sun-like star

Too hot

Just right

Too cold

▲ To support life, planets must be neither too near nor too far from their star.

About 22 per cent of Sun-like stars have Earth-sized planets in their Goldilocks zones.

Signs of life

Once an Earth-like Goldilocks exoplanet has been discovered orbiting a Sun-like star, scientists still face the difficulty of knowing whether the planet really does support life. So they are trying to work out what clues might tell them that life may already be present.

LOOKING AT ATMOSPHERES

One idea is to study the atmosphere of the exoplanets carefully. The light from the planet can be split into different colours to make a rainbow-like spectrum. The spectrum can then be examined to learn what the planet's atmosphere is made of and how hot it is. Scientists will be looking for signs that water vapour, ozone and carbon dioxide are present in the atmosphere.

Oxygen produced by plants and algae

Liquid water

Carbon dioxide given off by living organisms

Methane produced by living organisms

▲ Oxygen, water, methane and bacteria are tell-tale signs of life on the Earth.

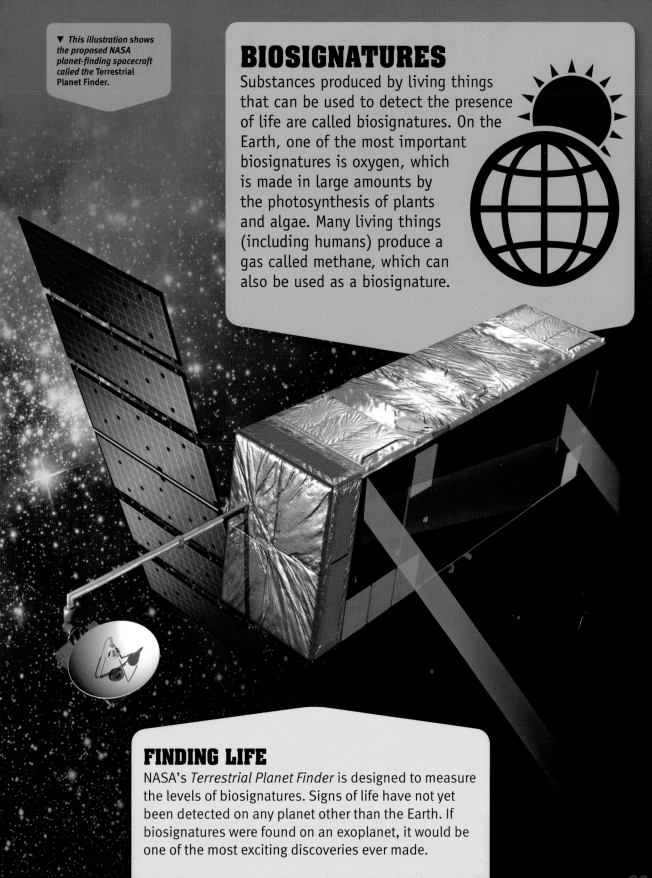

▼ This illustration shows the proposed NASA planet-finding spacecraft called the Terrestrial Planet Finder.

BIOSIGNATURES

Substances produced by living things that can be used to detect the presence of life are called biosignatures. On the Earth, one of the most important biosignatures is oxygen, which is made in large amounts by the photosynthesis of plants and algae. Many living things (including humans) produce a gas called methane, which can also be used as a biosignature.

FINDING LIFE

NASA's *Terrestrial Planet Finder* is designed to measure the levels of biosignatures. Signs of life have not yet been detected on any planet other than the Earth. If biosignatures were found on an exoplanet, it would be one of the most exciting discoveries ever made.

44

This is rocket science

Astronomers can explore the Universe in great detail by putting powerful telescopes into orbit around the Earth, and by launching spacecraft that can travel to bodies across the Solar System. This requires very advanced and expensive equipment to be sent safely into precise orbits in space.

PLATFORM AND PAYLOAD

All spacecraft are made of two main parts: a platform and a payload. The platform is a very strong but lightweight structure that includes the engine, fuel and main power supply for the spacecraft. The payload is the scientific equipment, such as cameras and measuring instruments.

BURNING FUEL

Rockets work by forcing gases out of the nozzle of an engine at high speeds. As the gases push hard downwards, the rocket moves in the opposite direction. A lot of fuel is needed to propel the rocket and overcome the pull of the Earth's gravity. The rocket has to reach 28,000 kilometres per hour to get into orbit.

Rocket powered
Rockets travel at 28,000 km per hour to escape the Earth's gravity (see above).

Station to station
Space stations have orbited the Earth since the 1970s (see page 65).

Gravity assist
Some spacecraft use planets to help them speed up (see page 66).

Future travel
Spacecraft of the future may be powered by fusion rockets (see page 67).

▼ *Operated by the European Space Agency, an Ariane 5 rocket takes off. Its huge fuel load means it weighs several hundred tonnes at this point.*

MISSION CONTROL

Once the spacecraft is in orbit, scientists need to communicate with it, using radio signals to operate it. Instructions or commands are sent from a mission control centre on the Earth to change the orbit of a **Space Shuttle**, steer a telescope or beam back images.

◀ *Flight controllers communicate with the crew of a Space Shuttle as it comes in to land.*

SPACE STATIONS

Since the early 1970s, astronauts have been working in orbiting laboratories called space stations. The stations are usually assembled over a period of time with parts delivered by rockets, which also carry the astronauts and supplies. At the end of their lives, most space stations re-enter the Earth's atmosphere and burn up.

▲ *Launched in 1998, the International Space Station is a joint project by the space agencies of the USA, Russia, Japan, Europe and Canada.*

Touchdown
Rosetta's lander was the first vehicle to touch down on a comet (see pages 68–69).

Catch up
In 2014, the spacecraft *Rosetta* went into orbit around a comet (see pages 68–69).

Moving through space

Space is vast. Although scientists have worked out several clever ways of speeding up spacecraft, it still takes years to travel to the outer reaches of the Solar System. As yet, we haven't developed the technology to reach the nearest star to the Sun, Proxima Centauri, which is nearly 100,000 times more distant than the farthest planet, Neptune.

▲ *The rocket carrying the New Horizons probe launched in 2006.*

GRAVITY ASSIST

Gravity assist is one of the most ingenious ways of getting spacecraft to travel faster. It involves flying a spacecraft close to a planet, then using the pull of the planet's gravity to speed it up. This kick from nature was used to get *New Horizons* to Pluto (see page 54). The rocket carrying the probe took a route past Jupiter, using the giant planet's gravity to accelerate it.

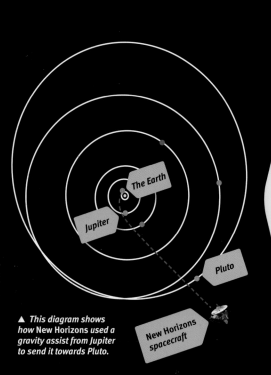

The Earth

Jupiter

Pluto

New Horizons spacecraft

▲ *This diagram shows how New Horizons used a gravity assist from Jupiter to send it towards Pluto.*

HELPING HANDS

Launched in 1997, the *Cassini* mission had four gravity assists on its 3.5-billion-km path to Saturn (see page 48). It was flown twice by Venus, and then past the Earth and Jupiter.

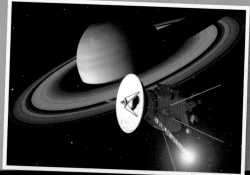

◄ *Even with four gravity assists, it still took Cassini seven years to reach Saturn.*

FUSION PROPULSION

Scientists are looking at new ways of powering future spacecraft. These include fusion propulsion, a new technology that could get spacecraft to travel faster through space. The engines of the new spacecraft would use bubbles of electrified gas and magnetic fields to make fusion energy – the same process that powers the Sun. The energy would vaporize metal, which would then be ejected out of the back of the spacecraft though a nozzle. This would create a lot of thrust, pushing the spacecraft through space at very high speeds.

Solar panel

▲ An artist's impression of a fusion propulsion rocket.

SOLAR SAILS

One way of accelerating spacecraft without carrying huge amounts of heavy fuel is to use solar sails. Just as a boat moves when wind pushes its sails, a spacecraft fitted with solar sails is pushed along by sunlight. The solar sail acts like a huge mirror. When light from the Sun falls on its shiny side and reflects, the spacecraft is pushed forward. Slowly, as more and more sunlight strikes the sail, the speed of the spacecraft increases greatly.

▶ In the future, we may be able to build solar sails several kilometres across that could help us travel to the stars.

How to land on a comet

In November 2014, a spacecraft landed on the surface of a comet for the first time. Carried out by the European Space Agency (ESA), the mission involved steering the *Rosetta* spacecraft on a ten-year journey through 6.5 billion kilometres of space. The goal of the mission was to study a comet up-close in order to improve our knowledge of the origin of the Solar System and its planets.

▼ *Rosetta's mission revealed the rough, jagged surface of the comet.*

TARGET COMET

Rosetta's mission was to catch up with a comet called 67P/Churyumov-Gerasimenko, far out in the Solar System. First, it made several close passes of the Earth and Mars using the gravity assist method to increase its speed (see page 66). This was very important as the comet was travelling at almost 64,500 kilometres per hour. When *Rosetta* finally reached the comet, the spacecraft was almost 510 million kilometres from the Earth.

INTO ORBIT

Launched in March 2004, *Rosetta* took just over a decade to reach its target. In August 2014, it went into orbit around the comet and began sending the most detailed images yet taken of a comet's surface. Comet 67P/Churyumov-Gerasimenko is about 4 kilometres wide and has a very rugged surface, with lots of sharp cliffs.

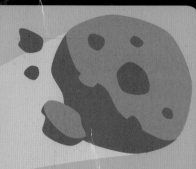

Rosetta's target, 67P/Churyumov-Gerasimenko, is as big as a mountain.

TINY LANDER

Rosetta was carrying a small landing probe called *Philae*, which it launched onto the comet's surface on 12 November 2014. Once it landed, *Philae* was meant to fire harpoons to fix it to the surface, but these failed to work. *Philae* bounced three times before settling in the shadow of a cliff, away from sunlight and without solar power. Its batteries only lasted a few hours before they ran down.

▲ *An artist's impression of how the* Philae *probe was supposed to land, out in the open.*

▲ *When 67P/Churyumov-Gerasimenko got close to the Sun and heated up, it began to expel the great clouds of gas and dust that make up its long tail.*

MAKING CONTACT

Philae still managed to complete a lot of the measurements it was meant to take. Scientists had hoped that, as the comet moved closer to the Sun, *Philae* might receive enough light to power up. It did briefly, but as the comet neared the Sun, it started to warm up and expel matter. This meant that *Rosetta* had to be steered several hundred kilometres away for its own safety. This put *Rosetta* too far from *Philae* to receive any more signals from the lander.

Eyes on the Universe

Telescopes are our eyes for viewing the Universe, allowing us to look at and learn about galaxies, stars, planets and other matter far off in space. Modern astronomers use extremely powerful telescopes to collect and study the light from these objects. Ever since Galileo turned one of the first telescopes towards the planets more than **400** years ago, we have been finding ways to see farther into the Universe, and in ever greater detail.

▲ *Located 4000 metres above sea level in Mauna Kea, Hawaii, USA, the Keck Observatory has two 10-metre telescopes.*

Stars near the centre of our galaxy zoom around at 5 million kilometres per hour.

Seeing farther
Powerful telescopes can reveal the Universe's depths (see pages 70–71)

Sky high
Telescopes on mountain tops help to avoid light pollution (see page 71)

Other wavelengths
Space telescopes pick up X-ray and infrared light (see pages 72–73)

Ground control
Giant telescopes made up of many dishes detect radio waves (see page 73)

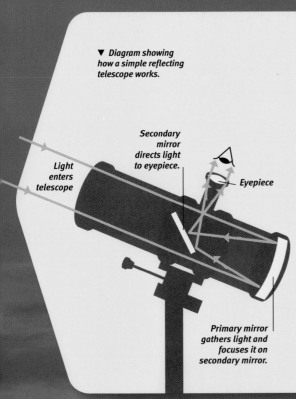

▼ *Diagram showing how a simple reflecting telescope works.*

Secondary mirror directs light to eyepiece.

Light enters telescope

Eyepiece

Primary mirror gathers light and focuses it on secondary mirror.

GATHERING LIGHT

A telescope collects the light from faraway stars and galaxies, then magnifies it to make faint objects appear brighter and closer. Most telescopes have two main parts. A primary mirror collects the light and brings it to a sharp point called a focus. Then, an eyepiece takes the light focused by the mirror and magnifies it to make a larger image. Telescopes that use mirrors are reflecting telescopes. Sometimes a lens is used instead to collect and focus the light – these telescopes are called refracting telescopes. The bigger the mirror or lens, the more light it can collect, which in turn makes the image brighter and sharper.

GIANT TELESCOPES

Today, astronomers use giant telescopes that can have primary mirrors up to 10 metres wide. These telescopes are kept in huge dome-shaped buildings called observatories, which also contain lots of other scientific equipment. Observatories are often situated in high, isolated locations in order to keep them away from city lights, which can interfere with the light coming from space. For instance, the European Southern Observatory in Chile is located 3000 metres above sea level in the mountains. Its incredibly powerful telescopes allow us to see objects that are 4 billion times fainter than can be seen just with the human eye.

▲ *Both of the Keck Observatory's telescopes have 36 small mirrors that work together like a big mirror.*

Hubble Telescope
Since 1990, *Hubble* has sent back amazing images of space (see pages 74–75).

Even farther
In the future, even more powerful telescopes will be built (see pages 76–77).

Seeing the invisible

The light we see is called optical or visible light, but it is just one type of light. Radio waves, infrared, ultraviolet, X-rays and gamma rays are also types of light, and together they make up the full range, which is called the electromagnetic spectrum. This range goes from low-energy light (radio waves) to high-energy light (X-rays and gamma rays). Many objects in the Universe give off these different types of light.

Electromagnetic waves are the only type of waves that can travel through space.

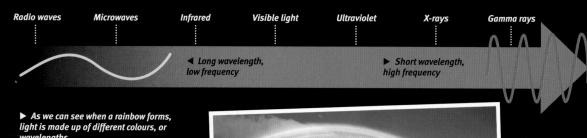

Radio waves | Microwaves | Infrared | Visible light | Ultraviolet | X-rays | Gamma rays

◄ Long wavelength, low frequency

► Short wavelength, high frequency

▶ As we can see when a rainbow forms, light is made up of different colours, or wavelengths.

▼ The Earth's atmosphere provides a protective blanket against the most harmful forms of light.

DETECTING LIGHT

Fortunately, the Earth's atmosphere protects us from X-rays and gamma rays, which can be harmful. However, this means that astronomers have had to launch telescopes into orbit to study objects emitting light in these wavelengths. To explore the hottest and most energetic stars, astronomers use X-ray and ultraviolet telescopes. Telescopes that detect infrared light are used to look at colder regions, such as clouds of gas and dust surrounding new stars.

VERY LARGE ARRAY

One of the world's most advanced radio telescopes is the Very Large Array (VLA). Located in the Socorro desert, New Mexico, USA, it is made of 27 radio dishes, each measuring 25 metres in diameter. These are linked together to make a very sensitive radio telescope.

▼ The VLA has made important observations of young stars and black holes.

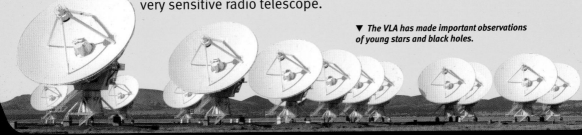

SEEING X-RAYS

A powerful space telescope called the *Chandra X-ray Observatory* was put into orbit in July 1999 by the Space Shuttle *Columbia*. Designed to study X-rays coming from far-off objects, *Chandra* has an oval-shaped orbit that takes it almost a third of the way to the Moon before returning it closer to the Earth. It can observe X-rays coming from hot gas clouds 5 million light years away.

▶ An artist's impression of the **Chandra X-ray Observatory**.

▼ Aerial view of the LIGO detector in Washington State, USA, showing its 4-km-long arms.

BRAND NEW WINDOWS

In February 2016, scientists at the LIGO laboratories in the USA detected the gravitational waves made by two black holes colliding 1.3 billion light years away. This confirmed the theory of space and gravity made 100 years ago by German scientist Albert Einstein.

Hubble glory

In April 2015, the *Hubble Space Telescope* marked its 25th anniversary of observing the Universe. It has been one of the most successful and long-lived of all space missions. This powerful telescope has beamed back thousands of images, providing us with amazing views of space.

NO ATMOSPHERE

The big advantage of putting a telescope into space is that it is above the Earth's atmosphere. This means that the light reaching the telescope is not blurred or blocked out by the atmosphere. A telescope that sits above the atmosphere has a much clearer view of the Universe.

AMAZING IMAGES

Hubble has changed the way we understand the Universe. Its data has revealed new information on how stars are made in gas clouds as well as how they change as they age. Scientists have used the telescope to figure out how galaxies formed when the Universe was young, and how they form clusters. *Hubble*'s data has even prompted discoveries about how the Universe is expanding faster and faster, which has led to new theories about dark energy.

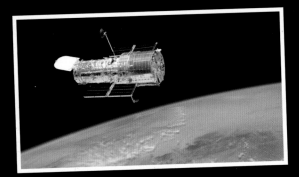

◀ Hubble, *one of history's most important scientific instruments, in orbit above the Earth.*

GIANT MIRROR

The *Hubble Space Telescope* was launched into orbit by the Space Shuttle *Discovery* in 1990. It orbits the Earth about once every 97 minutes at a height of 569 kilometres above the surface. *Hubble*'s main telescope mirror is 2.4 metres in diameter. The telescope is the length of a large bus and would weigh about 11,300 kilograms on the Earth.

SPECTROGRAPHS

Hubble is also fitted with spectrographs. A spectrograph splits the light from stars and galaxies into different colours to make a spectrum. Scientists can learn a great deal about an object in space by studying its spectrum, such as how hot it is and what gases it contains.

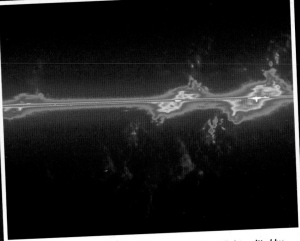

▲ An image taken by Hubble's spectrograph showing light emitted by a black hole at the centre of galaxy NGC 4151.

▶ This Hubble *image shows bubbles of ejected stellar material surrounding the central star of the Cat's Eye planetary nebula.*

◀ The swirling dust clouds in this Hubble *image surround the massive star V838 Monocerotis, which lies about 20,000 light years away from the Earth.*

▲ An astronaut performs a spacewalk during a service mission to the Hubble telescope.

SHUTTLE SERVICE

To keep it operating, *Hubble* was serviced five times between 1993 and 2009. Each time, astronauts replaced and upgraded its cameras, power units and optics. These re-fits helped to extend *Hubble*'s operating life by several years.

Future observatories

Scientists are designing the next generation of telescopes, which will provide us with the most detailed views of the Universe yet. However, these future telescopes will be very expensive to build, so the costs are being shared between many countries.

GATHERING MORE LIGHT

When completed in 2024, the E-ELT will be able to gather 13 times more light than the largest telescopes can today – that's 100 million times more light than enters the human eye. It's hoped that the E-ELT will make discoveries about the expansion of the Universe and how the first stars and galaxies formed.

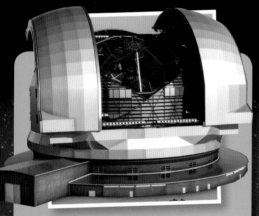

▲ An artist's impression of what the European Extremely Large Telescope will look like.

MOUNTAIN-TOP OBSERVATORY

Fourteen European countries plus Brazil are building the European Extremely Large Telescope, or E-ELT. To be located high up on a mountain in the Atacama Desert in Chile, the E-ELT will use a huge 39-metre-diameter mirror, made up of 798 hexagonal pieces.

The mirrors on the *JWST* are coated in gold to improve the reflection of light.

▲ Cerro Armazones, where the E-ELT will be built, offers clear views of the night sky.

▼ *Just a small section of the Square Kilometre Array in South Africa.*

RADIO GIANT

The Square Kilometre Array (or SKA) is being assembled in two main locations in South Africa and Western Australia. When complete in 2025, it will be the largest radio telescope ever built, with a light-collecting area of one square kilometre. Instead of a single dish to collect the radio waves, the SKA will combine the signal from thousands of small separate radio dishes or antennae. The SKA will be 10,000 times faster and 50 times more sensitive than the largest radio telescopes today.

BACK TO SPACE

NASA, ESA and the Canadian Space Agency are preparing the follow-up to the *Hubble* telescope. Called the *James Webb Space Telescope* (*JWST*), it is due to be launched in 2018 on top of an *Ariane 5* rocket. It will study the dawn of the Universe by detecting the faint heat from distant new stars.

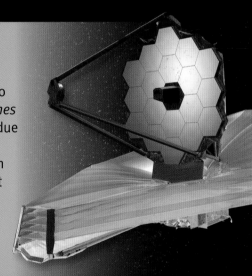

▶ *The mirror of the JWST will sit on top of a large sunshield, which will protect it from overheating.*

DISTANT EYES

The *JWST* has a 6.5-metre-diameter primary mirror, almost triple the size of *Hubble*'s mirror. It will be in orbit 1.5 million kilometres from the Earth, which is nearly four times further than the Moon.

▶ *A scientist checks part of the mirror during the telescope's construction.*

GLOSSARY

ASTEROID
A small, rocky body that orbits the Sun.

ASTRONAUT
Someone who travels into space on a spacecraft.

ASTRONOMER
A scientist who studies space.

ATMOSPHERE
The blanket of gases that surrounds some planets and bodies, including the Earth.

ATOMS
The smallest particle of a chemical element.

BIG BANG
The rapid cosmic expansion that marked the beginning of the Universe and the origin of space, matter, energy and time, according to the Big Bang Theory.

BLACK HOLE
A region of space where gravity has become so strong that nothing – not even light – can escape.

BODY
A naturally occurring object in space.

COMET
Small icy bodies found in the outer regions of the Solar System. Some comets have orbits that take them close to the Sun, causing them to heat up and release particles in the form of a long glowing tail.

DARK ENERGY
A mysterious force that has never been directly detected, but which many scientists believe accounts for most of the energy in the Universe, and is causing it to expand at an increasing rate.

DARK MATTER
An invisible type of matter that may make up about a quarter of the Universe.

ELEMENT
A substance with distinct characteristics that cannot be broken down into simpler substances. There are more than 100 elements, including hydrogen, helium, oxygen and carbon.

EXOPLANET
A planet that orbits a star other than our Sun, outside our Solar System.

GALAXY
A vast collection of stars, gas and dust held together as a single system by the force of gravity.

GRAVITY
The force that attracts bodies towards each other. The greater a body's mass, the greater its pull of gravity.

LANDER
A type of spacecraft designed to land on a planet, or other body, and investigate its surface and atmosphere.

LIGHT YEAR
A unit for measuring the vast distances of space. One light year is equal to the distance light travels in a year – around 9.46 trillion kilometres.

MATTER
A physical substance that occupies space and has mass.

MILKY WAY
The galaxy that contains the Solar System and is our home in the Universe.

NASA
The National Aeronautics and Space Administration, NASA, is the USA's main space agency, responsible for most of its space programmes.

NEBULA
A cloud of gas and dust where new stars are born.

NEUTRON STAR
The crushed, super-dense remnants of a star following a supernova.

NUCLEAR FUSION
The process in which two (or more) atomic nuclei from one element come together to form the nucleus of another element, releasing large amounts of energy. Stars shine because of nuclear fusion reactions.

ORBIT
To revolve around a body in space, held in place by gravity.

PROBE
A spacecraft that explores space.

ROVER
A manned or unmanned robotic vehicle used for exploring the surface of a planet or other body.

SOLAR SYSTEM
The Sun and all the bodies that orbit around it, including planets, dwarf planets, asteroids and comets.

SPACE SHUTTLE
A group of four NASA-built reusable spacecraft that flew a total of 135 missions between 1981 and 2011.

SUPERNOVA
The explosion of a massive star at the end of its life as a result of gravitational collapse.

TELESCOPE
A piece of equipment that makes distant objects appear closer and is used in the study of space.

X-RAYS
A type of high-energy light (or electromagnetism) emitted by some bodies in space, which can be detected by special telescopes.

INDEX

Picture credits (t=top, b=bottom, l=left, r=right, c=centre, fc=front cover, bc=back cover)

All images courtesy of NASA unless otherwise indicated.
European Southern Observatory (ESO): fc line 4r, 21br, 24br, 76cl. European Space Agency (ESA): 64–65c, 68–69c, 69br. LIGO: 73br. SKA Organisation: 77tl. German Aerospace Center: 69tr. Dreamstime: fc line 7cr, 6–7c, 7tr, 9c, 33tr, 55br, 62 c, cl, cr, bl, br, 70c, 72c, 73t. Shutterstock: 44b. Wikipedia Commons: 71br SiOwl. Public Domain: 4cr, 13tr, 16cl.